DINOSAURS

PREHISTORIC BEASTS

Per Christiansen

Gareth Stevens
Publishing

Please visit our web site at www.garethstevens.com
For a free color catalog describing Gareth Stevens Publishing's
list of high-quality books, call 1-800-542-2595 (USA)
or 1-800-387-3178 (Canada).
Gareth Stevens Publishing's fax: 1-877-542-2596

Library of Congress Cataloging-in-Publication Data
available upon request from publisher.

ISBN-10: 0-8368-9217-8 (lib. bdg.)
ISBN-13: 978-0-8368-9217-8 (lib. bdg.)

This North American edition first published in 2009 by
Gareth Stevens Publishing
A Weekly Reader® Company
1 Reader's Digest Road
Pleasantville, NY 10570-7000 USA

Copyright © 2009 by Amber Books, Ltd.
Produced by Amber Books Ltd., Bradley's Close
74–77 White Lion Street
London N1 9PF, U.K.

Illustrations © International Masters Publishers AB

Project Editor: James Bennett
Design: Tony Cohen

Gareth Stevens Senior Managing Editor: Lisa M. Herrington
Gareth Stevens Editor: Joann Jovinelly
Gareth Stevens Creative Director: Lisa Donovan
Gareth Stevens Designer: Paul Bodley

Printed in the United States of America

1 2 3 4 5 6 7 8 9 10 09 08

Contents

Argentavis	4
Borhyena	6
Brontotherium	8
Atlas Tortoise	10
Diatryma	12
Doedicurus	14
Giant Moa	16
Smilodon	18
Andrewsarchus	20
Giant Deer	22
Woolly Mammoth	24
Marsupial Sabertooth	26
Platybelodon	28
Glossary	30
For More Information	31
Index	32

Continents of the World

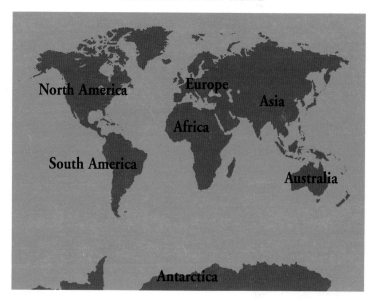

The world is divided into seven continents —
North America, South America, Europe, Africa,
Asia, Australia, and Antarctica. In this book,
the area where each animal lives is shown in red,
while all land is shown in green.

Words that appear in the glossary are printed in
boldface type the first time they occur in the text.

Argentavis

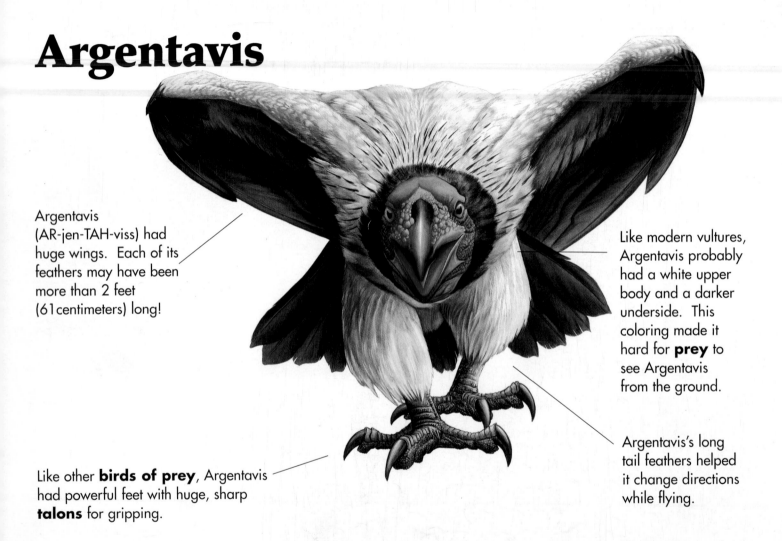

Argentavis (AR-jen-TAH-viss) had huge wings. Each of its feathers may have been more than 2 feet (61 centimeters) long!

Like modern vultures, Argentavis probably had a white upper body and a darker underside. This coloring made it hard for **prey** to see Argentavis from the ground.

Like other **birds of prey**, Argentavis had powerful feet with huge, sharp **talons** for gripping.

Argentavis's long tail feathers helped it change directions while flying.

Argentavis had a 21-foot (6.4-m) **wingspan**, more than twice as wide as today's largest flying bird, the Andes condor! Argentavis weighed about 155 pounds (70 kilograms).

Size

Argentavis belonged to a group of birds called condors, which live like vultures. Condors spend much of their time soaring high above the plains. They scan the horizon for carcasses with their sharp eyesight.

1 Argentavis swoops down to attack prey on the ground. The huge bird could kill animals quickly, including small horses.

2 Most of the time Argentavis probably dove from the sky to eat animals that were already dead. Like other birds of prey, it had a sharp beak, with a tip that curved downward. Its beak tore into the flesh of the **carcass**.

Where in the World

Argentavis lived in the mountains and wide, flat plains of Argentina about 6 million years ago.

5

Borhyena

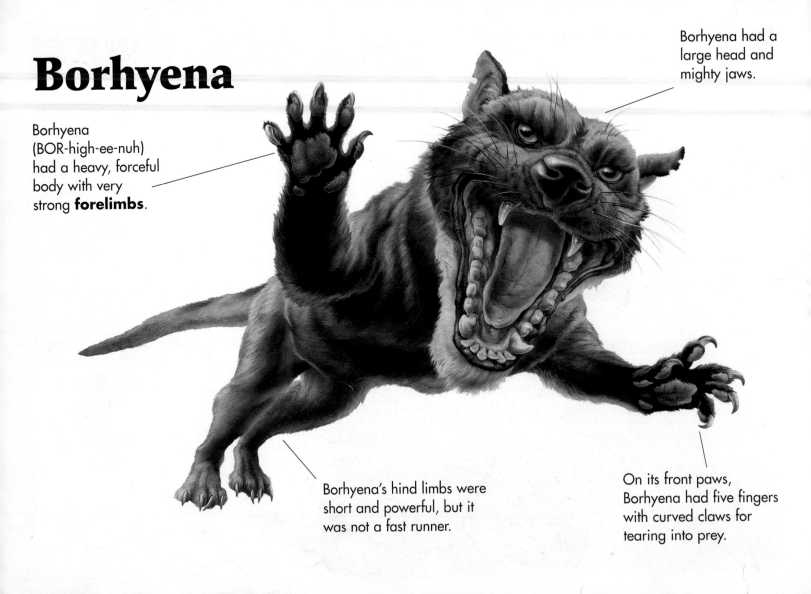

Borhyena (BOR-high-ee-nuh) had a heavy, forceful body with very strong **forelimbs**.

Borhyena had a large head and mighty jaws.

Borhyena's hind limbs were short and powerful, but it was not a fast runner.

On its front paws, Borhyena had five fingers with curved claws for tearing into prey.

Borhyena was the size of a wolf, but it was heavier and had shorter legs. It probably weighed around 200 pounds (91 kg), the same as a medium-sized black bear. Scientists believe that Borhyena hunted in packs.

Size

1 An advantage of pack hunting is that it allowed **predators** to kill large prey. A pack of Borhyena could bring down larger prey than a single animal could. Together, a pack of Borhyena were powerful enough to kill a young elephant! A pack could survive on this feast for weeks.

2 With Borhyena's incredibly strong jaws and teeth, it could crunch through bones with ease.

Where in the World

Borhyena and its relatives lived in the southern part of South America about 15 to 30 million years ago.

7

Brontotherium

Brontotherium (Bron-toe-THEE-ree-um) had a huge, bulky body. Its large stomach could **digest** tough plants, like rhinos do today.

Brontotherium's ears were large and cone-shaped, like those of a rhino. This shape sharpened sound, giving the animal excellent hearing.

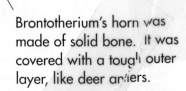

Brontotherium's horn was made of solid bone. It was covered with a tough outer layer, like deer antlers.

Brontotherium's legs were short and powerful, allowing it to reach speeds of 25 miles (40 kilometers) per hour.

Brontotherium was a huge, powerful beast. It stood more than 7 feet (2 m) tall and weighed more than 3 short tons (2.7 metric tons). Despite Brontotherium's large size, it could run fast and was nearly unstoppable!

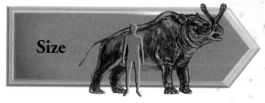

Size

1 Mature male Brontotheres had enormous, forked horns on their snouts that could reach a height of nearly 3 feet (9 cm). Here, two adults males fight over a female.

2 The strongest male rams his horn into the side of the other male, which then flees the scene.

Where in the World

Brontotherium and its relatives were a successful group of large plant-eaters. They lived in North America 30 to 40 million years ago.

Atlas Tortoise

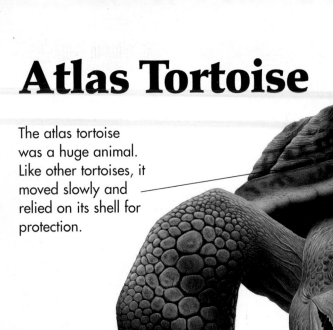

The atlas tortoise was a huge animal. Like other tortoises, it moved slowly and relied on its shell for protection.

A thick shell protected the atlas tortoise's soft body.

The atlas tortoise had a massive head. Its curved, horny beak was ideal for cropping plants.

The atlas tortoise's forelimbs were thick and strong. Tough scales covered its skin. The huge claws on this tortoise were great for digging up roots and **tubers**.

The atlas tortoise was the biggest tortoise that ever lived. Its shell was 8 feet (2.4 m) long, 5 feet (1.5 m) high, and it weighed around 2,000 pounds (907 kg).

Size

Tortoises are reptiles with scales, like snakes and lizards. Their scales have fused together, however, forming a huge shell. Most tortoises can pull their legs and head into their shell for protection. The opening is then blocked by its tough, scaly forelimbs.

1 The sabertooth tries to get at the juicy flesh of the tortoise.

2 The tortoise pulls back into its shell.

3 The tortoise is far too large and its shell much too strong for the sabertooth. It does make a good place to rest, though!

Where in the World

The atlas tortoise lived in India and on Indonesian islands around 7 to 12 million years ago.

11

Diatryma

The wings of Diatryma (Die-uh-TRY-mah) were tiny and useless for flying. This bird used its wings only to signal to other members of its **species**, like ostriches do today.

Diatryma had a mighty beak, which it used to tear flesh and crush bones!

Diatryma's long and powerful legs made it a speedy and dangerous predator.

Diatryma had huge, curved talons that grew from each of its three toes. It used them to rip into the flesh of its prey.

Diatryma was a frightening animal. Adults stood more than 7 feet (2.1 m) tall on long, powerful hind limbs. Diatryma's head was nearly as big as a small horse!

Diatryma may look like a giant ostrich, but it is actually related to birds called seriamas. Today these birds live in South America. Though seriamas fly well, they hunt mainly on the ground.

1 Diatryma was a fierce predator. It mainly fed on smaller animals, which it chased at high speeds.

2 Here, diatryma catches a horse-like animal. It snaps its prey's backbone with one, powerful bite!

3 Diatryma then begins to tear its prey into bite-sized chunks, using its massive beak. It holds tightly to its prey using its curved talons.

Where in the World

Diatryma and its close relatives lived in Europe and North America around 40 to 50 million years ago.

13

Doedicurus

A thick, strong shell formed by horny plates covered the body of Doedicurus (Doe-ED-ee-cue-russ). Mammals do not normally have hard shells, but armadillos and **pangolins** do.

Even the top of Doedicurus's head was covered in tough, bony plates. Predators found it difficult to bite through these plates.

Doedicurus's hind limbs were much weaker than its forelimbs. It could stand upright on its hind limbs to eat leaves.

Like today's armadillos, Doedicurus had very powerful forelimbs with huge claws for digging.

Doedicurus was a huge, tanklike animal. A massive shell covered its entire body. It was 10 feet (3 m) long from nose to tail and weighed about 1 short ton (907 kg). Its shell was so large that humans used it for a hut!

Close relatives of Doedicurus, the armadillos, are still common throughout the Americas. Armadillos also have armor and are skilled at digging with their clawed forelimbs. An animal as huge as Doedicurus probably dug up as much as 50 pounds (23 kg) of roots and tubers every day.

Doedicurus's shell offered protection against predators. But they also protected the animals from each other! Here, two males are engaged in a vicious fight over territory. They use their tail clubs for battering each other. Sometimes a shell broke from a hard blow, and the injured animal limped away in defeat. Scientists have found **fossils** of animals with broken shells and ribs.

Where in the World

Doedicurus lived in South America about 4 million years ago. The last animals died out only 10,000 years ago and shared their **habitat** with early humans.

15

Giant Moa

A giant moa's (MO-uh's) body looked almost furry, because its feathers were slender. Similar feathers are found on modern flightless birds, such as ostriches.

The giant moa had small wings and could not fly. Like ostriches, it used its wings only to communicate.

The giant moa ran fast on long, powerful legs. Its talons were blunt and used for scraping the ground.

The giant moa had a small head with a curved beak for nipping leaves. It was so tall that it could eat leaves from the tops of trees.

The giant moa is also called Dinornis, which means "terrible bird." These birds were peaceful plant eaters. Giant moas stood 12 feet (3.6 m) tall and weighed 500 pounds (227 kg)!

Size

Did You Know?

Giant moas became **extinct** less than 400 years ago. During the 1300s, the Maori people arrived in New Zealand. They began hunting the giant moas, which soon became rare. The last birds disappeared during the 1800s.

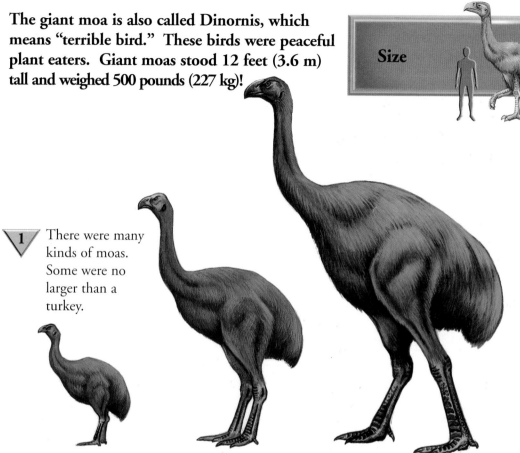

1 There were many kinds of moas. Some were no larger than a turkey.

Most moas were about 5 to 6 feet (1.5 to 1.8 m) tall. They looked like modern emus, which live in Australia. Moas had few predators besides giant eagles.

2 Giant moas probably grew larger to be able to digest tough plants. Digesting plants requires a large stomach and long **intestines**. Like today's turkeys, moas ground up the plants in a muscular **gizzard** filled with stones.

3

Where in the World

Moas lived only in New Zealand. They are related to kiwis, which still live on the islands today.

17

Smilodon

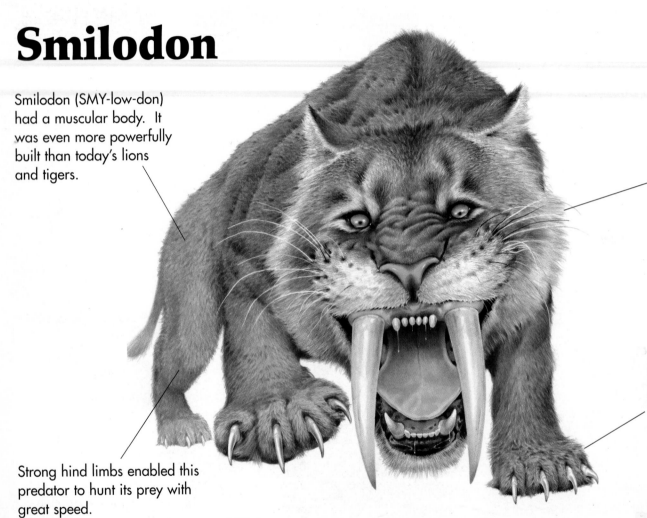

Smilodon (SMY-low-don) had a muscular body. It was even more powerfully built than today's lions and tigers.

Smilodon had a large head. Its extremely long upper **canine** teeth were shaped like the blade of a knife.

Smilodon had strong forelimbs, like all sabertoothed tigers. They also had huge, razor sharp claws for gripping prey.

Strong hind limbs enabled this predator to hunt its prey with great speed.

Smilodon was the size of a lion or tiger, but it was much more powerful. Large adult males weighed more than 500 pounds (227 kg). The North American Smilodon was smaller than the one living in South America.

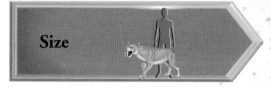

Size

Did You Know?

Smilodon was the last of a long-lived group of cats called the sabertooths. Early sabertooths lived about 10 to 12 million years ago. They were smaller and had much smaller teeth. Soon the sabertooths grew larger and sported huge upper canines.

1 A Smilodon attacks a big mammoth by gripping it with its powerful forelimbs and twisting itself underneath the beast's throat. Then it slashes the prey's throat with its huge fangs, killing it instantly.

2 Smilodon uses its huge upper teeth to tear a long gash into its prey's stomach before eating its flesh.

Where in the World

Smilodon lived in North and South America between 1 million and 10,000 years ago. Humans lived alongside the last of the Smilodons.

Andrewsarchus

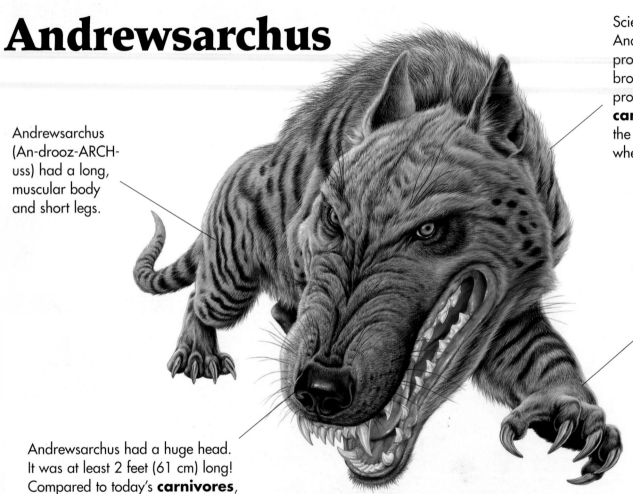

Scientists believe that Andrewsarchus probably had light-brown fur. Its fur provided good **camouflage** in the dry regions where it lived.

Andrewsarchus (An-drooz-ARCH-uss) had a long, muscular body and short legs.

This animal was not a fast runner. It relied on brute strength to kill prey.

Andrewsarchus had a huge head. It was at least 2 feet (61 cm) long! Compared to today's **carnivores**, Andrewsarchus was much larger.

Andrewsarchus was probably the largest carnivorous land mammal in history. It was more than 6 feet (1.8 m) tall and more than 13 feet (4 m) long. Its weight was nearly 1,000 pounds (454 kg)!

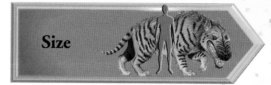

Size

1 Andrewsarchus was by far the largest and most powerful predator in its day. Since it moved slowly, it preyed on large plant-eaters, which were also slow moving. Andrewsarchus killed its prey by using force. Much of its diet was dead or injured animals.

2 Here, Andrewsarchus eats an injured **herbivore** lying helpless on the ground. The massive carnivore eats the plant-eater alive, ripping open its belly and feasting on its innards.

Did You Know?

Andrewsarchus is named after fossil hunter Roy Chapman Andrews. On his trips to Mongolia in the 1920s he also discovered fossils of Oviraptor and Velociraptor. Andrews even discovered the first fossilized dinosaur eggs.

Where in the World

Andrewsarchus was first found in Mongolia in 1923. Scientists have found very few fossils of Andrewsarchus.

Giant Deer

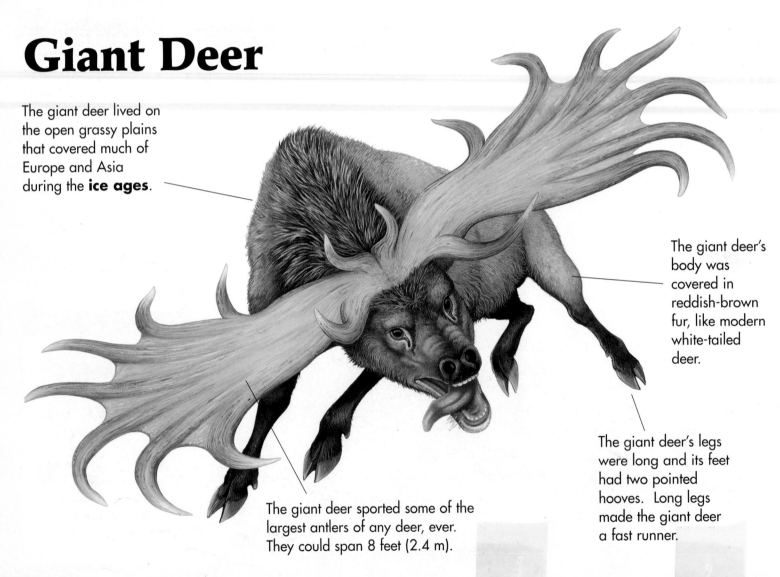

The giant deer lived on the open grassy plains that covered much of Europe and Asia during the **ice ages**.

The giant deer's body was covered in reddish-brown fur, like modern white-tailed deer.

The giant deer sported some of the largest antlers of any deer, ever. They could span 8 feet (2.4 m).

The giant deer's legs were long and its feet had two pointed hooves. Long legs made the giant deer a fast runner.

The giant deer is one of the largest species of deer that ever lived. Only the modern elk grows as big. Large stags stood almost 7 feet (2.1 m) at the shoulder and weighed more than 1,000 pounds (454 kg).

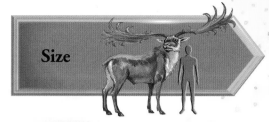
Two **stags** meet and try to scare each other by showing off their size. If this does not work, they will fight violently. The two stags lock horns and push and shove, attempting to defeat each other in a show of force.

Woolly Mammoth

The woolly mammoth had a tall, domed head like its close relative, the modern Indian elephant.

Like all mammoths, the woolly mammoth had enormous, curved tusks. Its long, powerful trunk ended in two wide, fingerlike tips.

The woolly mammoth was well adapted for cold ice age climates. Its thick woolly fur was covered by long hairs that grew up to 2 feet (61 cm) long.

Like today's elephants, the woolly mammoth had thick, straight legs to support its body.

The woolly mammoth was about the size of a modern Indian elephant. Males were 8 to 10 feet (2.4 to 3 m) tall and weighed between 5 to 6 short tons (4.5 to 5.4 m tons). Females were slightly smaller.

Size

Humans feasted on woolly mammoth meat during the last ice age, around 30,000 years ago. A kill was a rich source of food that saw a tribe through much of the harsh winter. Both early and modern humans hunted the woolly mammoth and cooked the meat over a roasting fire. They may have even lit fires inside the mammoth's body. Some scientists believe that it was over-hunting by humans that may have caused the mammoth to become extinct.

Did You Know?

The mammoth family was a group of elephants closely related to the modern Indian elephant. Mammoths had larger tusks than the Indian elephant. Its tusks were strongly curved. The woolly mammoth was the only mammoth that adapted to the cold northern climates.

Where in the World

The woolly mammoth lived throughout much of northern Europe, Asia, and North America during the last ice ages, between 150,000 and 10,000 years ago.

Marsupial Sabertooth

The marsupial sabertooth had a long, catlike body. Its short legs looked more like a bear's legs than a cat's. It was probably not a fast runner.

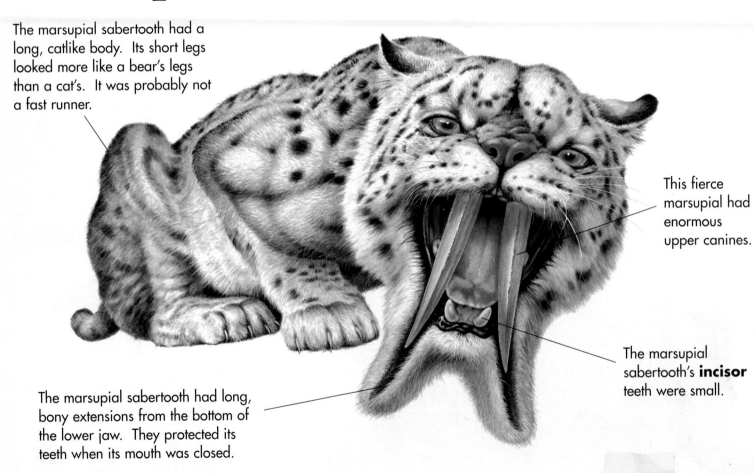

This fierce marsupial had enormous upper canines.

The marsupial sabertooth's **incisor** teeth were small.

The marsupial sabertooth had long, bony extensions from the bottom of the lower jaw. They protected its teeth when its mouth was closed.

The marsupial sabertooth was about 5 feet (1.5 m) long, including its tail. It weighed around 150 pounds (68 kg).

The marsupial sabertooth may have looked like a sabertooth tiger, but it was actually a marsupial. It was more closely related to kangaroos than to cats! Its closest relative was Borhyena, which also lived in South America.

1 A female marsupial sabertooth waits to **ambush** its prey near a water hole. When an animal comes to drink, the predator rushes out.

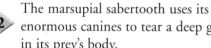

2 The marsupial sabertooth uses its enormous canines to tear a deep gash in its prey's body.

3 When its prey is dead, the mother calls for the kittens to come join the feast.

Where in the World

The marsupial sabertooth lived in Argentina between 2 and 7 million years ago.

Platybelodon

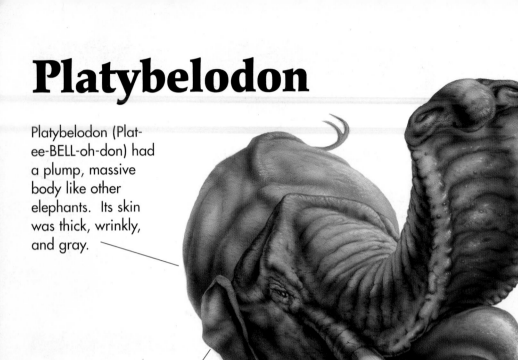

Platybelodon (Plat-ee-BELL-oh-don) had a plump, massive body like other elephants. Its skin was thick, wrinkly, and gray.

Platybelodon had a short trunk. Like modern elephants' trunks, it was a strong and important tool.

Like other elephants, Platybelodon had large ears, although not nearly as huge as those of modern African elephants.

Platybelodon's lower tusks were huge and flat. Like the upper tusks, they are huge incisor teeth!

Platybelodon was a medium-sized elephant. It was 7 to 8 feet (2.1 to 2.4 m) tall and weighed about 3 short tons (2.7 m tons). It lived in herds like modern elephants.

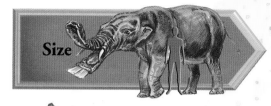

Size

Did You Know?

Platybelodon belongs to a group of elephants known as shovel-tuskers. Scientists are still not sure how they lived, but their fossilized tusks are often worn. The animals probably used them to dig in muddy ground.

1 There were many different kinds of elephants in Platybelodon's day. Anancus had straight tusks up to 13 feet (4 m) long, which it used for digging up tubers.

2 Cuvieronius had spiral tusks. It lived in the Americas until just 1,600 years ago.

3 Ambelodon was a close relative of Platybelodon. It used its lower tusks to dig up soft plants along lakes or rivers.

Where in the World

Platybelodon fossils have been found throughout much of the world.

Glossary

ambush — to make a surprise attack from a hiding place

birds of prey — birds that eat animals they have killed or that are already dead

camouflage — surface coloring that helps an animal blend in with the plants, rocks, and soil where it lives

canine — a cone-shaped pointed tooth

carcass — a body of a dead animal

carnivores — a meat-eater

digest — to break down food in the stomach so it can be used by the body for energy

extinct — when there are no more of a species left alive

forelimbs — the front legs or arms of an animal

fossils — the remains of a plant or animal that have been preserved in rocks that are found beneath Earth's surface

gizzard — a bird's tough, lower stomach that crushes and grinds food

habitat — a place where a plant or animal lives

herbivore — a plant-eater

ice ages — periods when Earth was covered by glacial ice

incisor — a front tooth for cutting food

intestines — parts of the body through which digested food passes after it leaves the stomach

marsupial — an animal with a pouch for carrying its babies

pangolins — animals from Asia or Africa that have large, horny scales that overlap

predators — animals that hunt and kill other animals for food

prey — animals hunted for food

species — a group of living things of the same family or type

stags — adult male deer

talons — sharp claws shaped like big hooks

tubers — short thick stems with tiny leaves that grow underground

wingspan — the measurement of a flying creature's wings from the end of one wingtip to the end of the other

For More Information

Books

Beyond the Dinosaurs: Sky Dragons, Sea Monsters, Mega-mammals, and Other Prehistoric Beasts. Howard Zimmerman (Atheneum, 2001)

The Complete Guide to Prehistoric Life. Tim Haines and Paul Chambers (Firefly, 2007)

Digging for Bird Dinosaurs: An Expedition to Madagascar. Scientists in the Field (series). Nic Bishop (Houghton Mifflin, 2002)

Dinosaurs: Prehistoric Creatures in the Sea & Sky. Nature's Monsters (series). Brenda Ralph Lewis (Gareth Stevens, 2006)

Dinosaurs: The Most Complete Up-to-Date Encyclopedia for Dinosaur Lovers of all Ages. Dr. Thomas R. Holtz, Jr. (Random House Books For Young Readers, 2007)

First Dinosaur Encyclopedia. Caroline Bingham (DK, 2006)

Web Sites

Dinosaur Facts
www.dinosaurfact.net

Ice Age Mammals – EnchantedLearning.com
www.enchantedlearning.com/subjects/mammals/Iceagemammals.shtml

National Museum of Natural History – Ice Age Mammals
www.mnh.si.edu/museum/VirtualTour/Tour/First/IceAge/index.html

Paleontology Portal
www.paleoportal.org

Prehistoric Animals – After the Dinosaurs
www.search4dinosaurs.com/prehistoric.html

University of California Museum of Paleontology (UCMP)
www.ucmp.berkeley.edu/index.php

Index

African elephants 28
Andrewsarchus 20–21
Andrews, Roy Chapman 21
antlers 22, 23
Argentavis 4–5
Argentina 5, 27
armadillos 14, 15
Asia 22, 23, 25
atlas tortoise 10–11

beak of
    Argentavis 5
    diatryma 12
    giant moa 16
Borhyena 6–7, 27
Brontotherium 8–9

camouflage of, Andrewsarchus 20
coloring of
    Argentavis 4
    giant deer 22
    condors 5

diatryma 12–13
doedicurus 14–15

ears of
    Brontotherium 8
    Platybelodon 28
elephants
    African 28
    Platybelodon 28, 29
    shovel tuskers 29
Europe 22, 23
extinction of
    giant moa 17
    woolly mammoth 25

feathers of
    Argentavis 4
    giant moa 16
feet of, Argentavis 4
forelimbs of
    Andrewsarchus 20
    atlas tortoise 10
    Borhyena 6
    doedicurus 14, 15
    Smilodon 18
fighting
    Brontotherium 9
    doedicurus 15
fur 22, 24

giant deer 22–23
giant moa 16–17
gizzard, giant moa 17

head of
    Andrewsarchus 20
    atlas tortoise 10
    Borhyena 6
    diatryma 13
    giant moa 16
    Smilodon 18
    woolly mammoth 24
    horn, Brontotherium 8, 9

ice age 22, 24, 25
India 11
Indian elephant 25
Indonesia 11
intestines, giant moa 17

jaws of
    Borhyena 6, 7
    marsupial sabertooth 26

legs of
    Brontotherium 8
    diatryma 12
    giant deer 22
    giant moa 16
    marsupial sabertooth 26
    woolly mammoth 24

marsupial sabertooth 26–27
Mongolia 21

New Zealand 17
North America 9, 19, 21, 25

ostriches 16
Oviraptor 21

Paltybelodon 28–29
predators of
    Borhyena 7
    diatryma 13
prey of
    Andrewsarchus 21
    Argentavis 4, 5
    Borhyena 6
    diatryma 13
    marsupial sabertooth 27

rhinoceros 9

sabertooth tiger 18
scales, atlas tortoise 10, 11
shell of
    atlas tortoise 10, 11
    doedicurus 15
size of
    Andrewsarchus 21
    Argentavis 5

atlas tortoise 10, 11
Borhyena 7
Brontotherium 9
diatryma 13
doedicurus 15
giant deer 23
giant moa 17
marsupial sabertooth 27
Platybelodon 29
Smilodon 19
woolly mammoth 25
skin, Platybelodon 28
Smilodon 18–19
South America 7, 15, 19, 21, 27

talons of
    Argentavis 4
    diatryma 12, 13
    giant moa 16
teeth of
    Borhyena 7
    marsupial sabertooth 26, 27
    Smilodon 18, 19
tusks of
    Platybelodon 28, 29
    woolly mammoth 24, 25

Velociraptor 21
vultures 5

wings of
    Argentavis 5
    diatryma 12
    giant moa 16
    woolly mammoth 24–25